Discovering My

Bears

by Melvin and Gilda Berger

SCHOLASTIC INC.

New York Toronto London Auckland
Sydney Mexico City New Delhi Hong Kong

ISBN 978-0-545-24439-8

Copyright © 2010 by Melvin & Gilda Berger

All rights reserved. Published by Scholastic Inc.
SCHOLASTIC and associated logos are trademarks
and/or registered trademarks of Scholastic Inc.

12 11 10 9 8 7 6 5 4   11 12 13 14 15/0

Printed in the U.S.A.   40
First printing, September 2010

Photo Credits:

Cover: © M. Watson/Ardea.com; Back cover: © Rolf Kopfle/Ardea.com; Title Page: © Lior Rubin/photolibrary; Page 3: © Chris Wallace/Alamy; Page 4: © Corbis Super (RF)/Alamy; Page 5: © CLFProductions/Shutterstock; Page 6: © Wild Wonders of Europe/Nature Picture Library; Page 7: © GlowImages (RF)/Alamy; Page 8: © Biosphoto/Photolibrary; Page 9: © Thomas Kitchin & Victoria Hurst/Getty Images; Page 10: © Robert Caputo/Getty Images; Page 11: © Linda Freshwaters Arndt/Photo Researchers, Inc.; Page 12: © John Pitcher/Corbis; Page 13: © Suzi Eszterhas/Nature Picture Library; Page 14: © BIOS/photolibrary; Page 15: © blickwinkel/Alamy; Page 16: © Jenny E. Ross/Corbis

Bears live in the forest.

Bears are very big.

What color is this bear's fur?

They have thick fur.

Bears are fast runners.

All winter, it sleeps in a den.

Baby cubs are born in the den.

The mother keeps the cubs warm.

In spring, the cubs come out to play.

Can the cubs climb high?

Climbing trees is a lot of fun.

Ask Yourself

1. Where do bears live?
2. What keeps bears warm?
3. How do bears move about?
4. What kind of food do bears eat?
5. Where are baby cubs born?

You can find the answers in this book.